Diaries of a "DRAMA" QUEEN!

keep u..!
Shining .

THE BIG START!

ASHIRAI NDORO

I

This book is a publication of
Billionaire Publishers
Website: marshalchiza.com

Editing by **Vonayi Nyamazana**
Typesetting by **Marshal Chiza**
Book Cover Design by **Diligent Palmer**

AcKnowledgements

I would like to thank my mom, who keeps encouraging me to believe in myself and follow my dreams. I have always wanted to write and publish a book since she became an author, and this is one of the best birthday presents ever! I also thank God for inspiring me to write this and reminding me that all things are possible when you believe they are. I am eager to follow my dreams. They are waiting for me just to go on and live them out!

I also want to thank my year four teacher Mr Grimditch for fuelling my creativity and supporting me with my writing.

Really grateful to my publisher Marshal Chiza who was very patient with me. You are the best publisher ever! Aunty Voni for being so amazing and helping me to get across my thoughts and ideas clearly.

Introduction

Welcome to my first diary. A place where I share my thoughts and activities and where if you are going to be allowed in, you have to promise to keep your mouth shut! I do not like snitches. Some people think that I am a drama queen, but I disagree with them. I am going to give you a run-down of the house so that you know who's who. I have put some abbreviations that I use at the beginning just to make sure you stay clued up, stick with the script; you know what I mean?

Welcome to my space. If you keep your lips pursed, then you will enjoy more of my secrets.

Share this book with your friends if you like it, follow me on social media, but for now, sit back and enjoy the read!

Harper Riley Quinn

Who's Who List

Harper Riley Quinn -That' s me, this is my diary

Marley aka Marles -My little sister

Mom and dad -"The Parents", self-explanatory

Payton -My big sister

Xavia Degrange -Payton' s friend

Teagan -Xavier' s daughter

Everleigh -Xavier' s daughter

Asia -Xavier' s daughter

Kylie and AJ (Alyssa Javance) -My BFFs, at least I think so

Reagan and Oliver -AJs twin siblings

Paige McKinley	—My arch enemy
Yasmin	—Paige' s little sister
Charlotte	—Paige' s original squad member
Jennifer Puddington	—Paige's squad
Hannah	—Paige' s friend
Liam McAllister	—Cute boy in class
Mr Talop	—Dance teacher
Miss Jones	—Class teacher
Miss Liles	—French teacher
Chahal Renis	—Lame TV show host

Abbreviations

BFF	–Best friend forever
BFFAE	–Best friends forever and ever
BTW	–By the way
CAPGHO	–Cool and popular girls hang out
FYI	–For your information
HTNG	–How to not get
MLC	–Miss Liles Class
MPPCI	–Most prized possession confiscated in
OMG	–Oh my gosh
SPD	–Super private diary
TBH	–To be honest

The Big Start

Saturday June 20th

OMG, I can' t believe what is happening to me!

1- I have been transferred to a new school!

2- A mean bully goes there according to what is blowing up on my Insta feed!

You can keep reading if you keep quiet about this diary and don' t have a potty mouth like Marley. My little sister who has a full-time job as my snitch!!!

Her salary will be dishes duty tonight! (if I' m lucky enough to be in charge of the chores rota)

BTW. If you know you cannot keep quiet, then please, pretty please return this to Harper Riley Quinn UNOPENED!

Sorry, I have some stuff to organise, you' ll find out all about it later. I' ll finish this tomorrow. I' m on the last stretch of summer break, so I don' t have much time to spend on this tonight.

Sunday, June 21st

Hmm, where did I finish off last night? Okay, so! I was at one of my BFF's place.

Well, Kylie's home to be specific. I was at Kylie's because Alyssa's toddler twin siblings, Reagan and Oliver were driving Alyssa's mum and dad crazy!

Kylie, Alyssa and I had called a few other people because we were rehearsing for Mr Talop's dance recital.

He had auditions for a female dancer to duet with my crush, Liam McAllister! Can you believe that? I have got to get that part! I hear Paige really likes him too. Thank goodness summer club got me acquainted fully with who's who at this new turf.

I mean seriously, any random snoopers really need to get out of my diary because *(yawns)* you tattletales are lucky because I' m way too tired to fight you today.

Monday, June 22nd

OMG!!! What in the whole of Paige McKinley's house is going on?

Sorry, I say things or people I hate when I'm mad. In particular, Paige, who claims that her great great great grandad is William McKinley. Always wanting a stake to claim some fame!

Her nosy friend Hannah who always keeps straight A' s in history, must have helped her out to attain her A grades. There would be no way the teachers would have gotten tricked into;

1- Giving her perfect grades.

2- Giving her the cheerleading team captain seat.

3- And making her class president before I even arrived on the scene! All that good stuff on one person? So not fair!

She does not seem to like me and is living my dream life! Now you see why she is not my best friend. I cannot stand it!

Oops, sorry the news is out now!

I have to get focused; SCHOOL IS STARTING TOMORROW! New school and I have to bring my best personality forward.

Good to have had a head start in getting to know about everyone as well as making some friends during summer. That credit goes to my friend AJ for giving me the all the "hot tea" on the happenings around here. Thank goodness for the teacher training day that has helped me wind down from the summer break! Time to face the world!

I'm just going to blurt this out now! Warning all snoopers who are going to share this information, i.e.

Marley (she usually gets tempted to get into my stuff then goes on to tell EVERYBODY!).

WARNING!

This diary is filled with my private thoughts and secrets.

DO NOT TOUCH !!!

I have a tincey wincey crush on Liam! I saw him playing basketball on the courts with his friends! Apparently, he always gets the male lead in plays. I have to get that part in that dance musical! How cool would that be?

Tuesday, June 23rd

So today the plan is to sneak my diary into class and not get it confiscated. Simple enough, right? I'm really taking a big chance by writing in it now whilst in class.

Sorry, Marley has just walked into my class and is screaming her head off. I wonder what that's all about?

Marley: Why do I have to get into trouble on the first day in school?

Me: Really, Marles?

Marley: Yeah, my toy got confiscated. And it was a fidget spinner.

Me: (looks around at class and then speaks) Fidget spinners were out like two years ago Marley, so cry me a river, build me a bridge and get over it!

Oh boy! I love my little sister BUT! Don' t ask. Siblings can have a way of embarrassing you in front of your whole class! That memory of me is likely going to stick in everyone's mind as the others form an impression of me.

Note to self:
Don' t forget the HTNG MPPCI MLC.
(How to not get most prized possession confiscated in Miss Liles class!)
Not sure I am going to enjoy French. It never was one of my strong languages.

Thursday, June 25ᵗʰ

Yep. That, "sneak my diary into the class" plan did not work! It got taken from me for one whole day! I guess that means no entry on Wednesday the 24th! SHOUT OUT TO PAIGE MCKINLEY FOR THAT! Teacher's pet and snitch extraordinaire!

Now you got what you want, Paige. Now the world will know your name but for a completely different reason since my little sister Marley, is publishing this diary. I know once she gets a hold of any information, she cannot help but repeat it! Get this, if my sister publicises the information in this diary, everyone will know Paige is a bully and snitch and wants to be ruler of everything.

They might then avoid her like the plague, and maybe I will be able to get hold of some of the luxury spots she has already taken! How does one get into all the positions someone else has already claimed when you are the new kid in school?

Marley's "potty mouth" might well end up being really useful. Now I don' t have anything against Marley. P.S my sister rules!

Note to self:

Remember dance auditions later today.
I need to get that part!

Friday, June 26ᵗʰ

I am one day ahead of the game and this all happened yesterday. Okay, I went to the dance auditions, blah blah blah.... yeah. Oh, I forgot that mum said next Wednesday, Marley and I would be missing school because Payton is coming home. Payton is our older sister, who is now a fashion designer.

Then it so happened that the day of the first dance rehearsal was announced to be on the day that Payton is coming.

You see, my dream has come true, and I have been selected to do the duet with Liam. I had gotten so muddled up with dates I had told Paige (who was in control of deciding the days of rehearsal) that my big sister Payton was coming over next Thursday.

In an attempt to put me in an awkward position and force me to reject the duet role, Paige's eyes filled with deviousness, and she announced, "I will be having the first meeting as class president on Wednesday, so the first performance will have to be on Thursday. Anyone who cannot make it and has a role or part to play needs to relinquish their position by the close of day tomorrow and inform the teacher so they can select an alternative person for the role! If it is an important role, then that would be ME!"

You see what I mean? Like who in their right mind does that?

It was so good to offload all these happenings to Kylie today!

Saturday, June 27th

OMG, you will NEVER understand how I've been improving in dance, I really want to play that role! But on the flip side because of all the attention I had been giving it, I' ve been failing in everything else. Mum says that if I don' t start getting my grades up, I get my phone confiscated for a week! At least I still have a good role to look forward to!

Good job I had got the dates wrong about the first rehearsal. Thank goodness I won' t have to be around to listen to Paige' s dumb speech. Can you imagine her face when I show up to take the lead duet role on Thursday? Her eyes will be full of envy when I take the solo too!

Note to self:

Meet Kylie and AJ (Alyssa Javance' s short name that Kylie and I call Alyssa when we forget her full name!)
at the CAPGHO.
(Cool and popular girls hang out!)

Sunday, June 28th

Hello, it's Harper Riley Quin, not Marley. I love dolls, and at my preschool, I mean big girl school, I have no more break. I saw my last page and realised how dumb and silly my silly diary sounds. I wish I had a rubber, but I cut it up to make drinks for my barbie's. Hold on, let me get my cute reporter girl Marley.

Let me tell you the truth. I am Marley Summer Quin, and I will be telling you my biggest secret. I am going to publish this diary. Also, my sister Harper told me I could tell you that she picks her nose and eats it. Ha ha ha! She can be such a Loser!

Monday, June 29th

OMG Marley, you are in so much trouble, girl! Wait till I catch you with my diary again. That is another diary day entry lost! I'm just praying that my little sister turning my rubber into toy drinks is a dream. Argh, she got them into such tiny pieces that my mum vacuumed them up when she was cleaning.

Seriously, somebody, please pinch me and tell me that I'm dreaming. I need to wake up from this nightmare! Now Marley knows all my secrets!

Goodness me! This bad feeling brings back memories of when one of Paige's squad members, (now ex squad member) called Charlotte met me for the first time with my Taylor Swift shirt on and said: "Taylor was so out last week, someone needs to wake you up!" And she poured water all over my branded top!

Then Kylie stood up for me and yelled: "Stinky attitude was out about a second ago, so I think you will find that it is you who needs to be awakened!"

24

"Ugh, I am awake!" Charlotte squealed, fanning herself with a fluorescent hot pink fan with rose gold ruffles and binged out with magenta rhinestones.

Tuesday, June 30th

Me, AJ, Kylie and Marley again, don' t ask! What? I can' t have my snitch blabbering on me! Sorry, I got a bit distracted there. A bit?

Argh, I'm doing it again. But seriously do I have some sort of disease of getting distracted? Like in Miss Jones class when I got so tired after a late night of chatting with AJ about her sister Reagan throwing up after Oliver shoved a full, exactly 5 ½ inch tablespoon of canned tuna into Reagan's mouth! We laughed so hard and went to bed close to ten o'clock! I told mum I was reading, but I'm sure she heard the giggling on the phone.

I somehow managed to start dozing off in class which drew the attention of the teacher. She intercepted one of the notes we had been passing to each other as AJ was caught trying to nudge me for a response by tossing a note rolled up in my face and waking me up. AJ and I got detention, and the teacher thankfully put us in the same room. Not the kind of reputation you want to build in a new school, but hey, at least I had a friend in with me too.

So AJ and I were in detention, talking about how Miss Jones should go back to preschool, loosen up and try and have some fun. We joked and laughed, raising our voices a little too high such that Miss Jones overheard us. We think that is why she found a way to fail us both in the homework that we had submitted. Just what I need right now! NOT!

See how I get way too carried away sometimes?

Breathe.... At least I managed to get my other grades up today!!!

Wednesday, July 1st

Okay, right now I am in the car driving to the airport to pick up Payton, but I did not go to the special meeting at the CAPGH! Great! Just great!

Just to make my day better, I got a text that AJ joined the CAPGH! Paige's crew. How could she?

AJ was one of my best friends back in Georgia. She moved out of her state to be with me, and now she was against me? For some reason, I had Paige's number just to leave very annoying messages on her line. I decided to call her and told her how it was all her fault I was not able to be at the special meeting, but she just whispered, "blame the mother dear." then hung up. I just sat there in the car. Felt like I was in a bad dream because I could not believe all of the bad things that were happening to me all at once! This one had cost me one of my BFF's.

"Isn't it a bit of your fault Harper? One, you missed the meeting and two, you interrupted Paige's speech." Marley said to me.

OMG, you will not believe how proud my parents seemed to be of Marley and how their youngest had managed to bring me down to size!

So, I could not help but reply in a rather loud voice, "It is mostly your fault for making me deal with the diary drama. And have I not told you to stop eavesdropping? It's rude!"

Then typical to her behaviour, Marley started jeering and pulling faces, eager to start a fight with me!

She yelled "YOU ARE THE MEANEST GIRL ON EARTH," so loud the car echoed! Then dad gave us each a smack on our knees from the passenger seat.

"That is disgraceful behaviour! Stop it now!" He said in his serious voice.

He even managed to resist Marley' s puppy face, which is usually so cute and causes him to cave in and melt. " Whose children, are you? Who is influencing you to behave like this?"

" You!" I said moodily.

" Watch your mouth Miss Smartie. That attitude could get you grounded for a whole week!"

33

This time no one argued or even spoke. Even Marley shut up, which is usually impossible. We could all feel that tensions were running high! In fact, the tension in the air was so thick that you could feel it and mom who was driving, visibly slowed the car and gave dad a quick look that begged him to calm down before she stepped hard on the pedal again.

However, he was not letting anything cool him down!

He just held his hand out and wagged his index finger at Marley just in case she said a stupid thing. (She usually always does!)

Sorry, I'm exhausted and have to go! No more writing for me today. I do not even have the energy to lock my diary! Bless Payton who has had to arrive into this sort of drama. It is nice to be back home, bedtime for me.

You, ha-ha take that Harper!

I will eat my veggies!

OH MY

I love daddy.

But mummy is better.

"Mum, dad, Marley stop writing in my SPD super-private diary!" Who has control of the diary now, hahaha! My arm is sore, and I can't write anymore.

OKay sweetKins, but daddy loves you.

Mummy gives you candy. I am Marley, and I can write wherever I want to.

Thursday, July 2nd

It is nice to have Payton home again. I'll give you a sneak peek of Payton's diary later. She has such an exciting life in the world of fashion as a designerS and she lets me read it myself whenever she comes home so I can get some insight into her world. Her arrival yesterday had temporarily broken the tension, and her sunny personality had warmed us all up to talking to each other in a friendly way again. It was so good to see her and hear about all that she had been up to.

Mum, dad, Marley, Payton and I were rushing to get to my performance rehersal that I absolutely had to make in order not to forfeit my position, when you will never guess what happened! A car crash! Of all the times for this to happen!

I will have to show you my older sister's diary next chapter because guess where she is now?

Hospital! Yes, can you imagine that!

Guess who caused the accident? Paige's dad!

He was speeding behind us and thought we were going to stop, but when we stopped at the red light, he kept surging forward towards us and hit us at the back! That is right near the spot Payton had been sitting! Paige literally confessed it with her own mouth as she 'apologised' that her dad, had hurt Payton! I know it was intentional!

I DEFINITELY SMELL A RAT!

👑 FRIDAY JULY 3rd

I decided to quit the school musical show before I got
disqualified anyway for missing the rehersal because of
the accident. Besides. Payton's doctor said she had
managed to break her leg and would get better quicker
if she was given very special attention! I keep telling

Marley to take her dangerous toy objects out of the car because they are a hazard! Poor Payton's leg had gotten caught up in one of Marley's contraptions during the impact!

My big sister was more important to me, and until she got better, I did not want to do anything that would stop me from helping her do so. It had also gotten complicated with Paige admitting what her dad did. I mean what sort of people were they?

Guess who showed up at the hospital and dropped off a drink at my sister's bedside table. Yep, none other than Paige in a "kind gesture" because of the remorse she felt! A drink that I think was aimed to poison her. Okay, now that may be a bit too dramatic, but she surely could not have meant her any good!

Well, at least that's what I think. Payton started swelling up soon after taking the dangerous drink, and it only took a few minutes for her face to start puffing up. The emergency buzzer had to be rung, and some special medicine had to be injected into her arm to stop the swelling. She has a lot of allergies, and the nurse had not checked this before pouring out the "grape juice" Paige had brought in.

As soon as she had heard the news, which was only today because we were all too shook up yesterday, Kylie came to the hospital too, which was really sweet. She wants to be a doctor herself one-day and dreams about graduating from Med school. She would never miss any legitimate opportunity to go to a hospital! Cray-cray! Not the most fun place to hang out if you ask me.

Anyway, an hour or so after Kylie arrived, the doctor said Payton was doing much better now and that she just needed another shot, the cast on her leg examined, then she was free to check out of the hospital!

Kylie had told me that Paige had apparently called for a dance battle contest and it was open to all for registration at 10 am sharp at the Layndoor Hotel the next day. She would perform with her little sister Yasmin (Marley's BFFAE best friends forever and ever). I do not even know how that happened; of all the people for Marley to decide to get on with, Paige's little sister. The minute I heard that news, I knew I had to form a team to contend with her on this!

Payton's friend Xavia came to pick us up from the hospital with her three children, and as I heard her talk about their performance achievements, right there, I had an aha moment.

Teagan, who is 6, Everleigh-five and Asia who is three, were all accomplished contest winners. Asia had entered 39 dance contests and has won them all. Tegan was literally a full-time actress, home-schooled by her mom, and at that tender age, Eveleigh is a pro rapper who has 120 shiny gold and silver trophies from numerous competitions she has won. All in one family, claiming top positions!!!

I decided to ask Xavia if her daughters could join my new formed dance team to compete in Paige's dance battle. With all this experience and expertise, we were going to take Paige down! Teagan had a current acting gig and would not be able to join us.

I could begin to smell the sweet smell of victory already!

Paige, you asked for this. We are coming for you hard! Harder than you have had it EVER BEFORE!!!

Saturday July 4th

That's how I was going to get that popularity vote and show Paige who she was messing with. A dance battle would do the job. I sent her a text message about registering and of course, she had to say yes!

like which mean, Chanel 5 perfume owner who gets uniform mail every-day and apparently has lipstick from the owner of Chanel (*who died like 600 years ago*) plus claims that she is descending from a former US president, would be able to turn down an entrance request into her dance battle with her chief rival? Right!

I decided to ask Xavia if she could drop off her daughters so they could start rehearsing before the big Independence day BBQ in the park this afternoon. "Competition" was their middle name and she was happy to bring Eveleigh to do the rap for us while Asia could do the dance choreograph. A wonderful surprise was that Teagan was also available and could join us.

They finally arrived just after 9 am, and Kylie (she had arrived at my place at 8:30 am and I rushed downstairs to meet them when guess who turned up?

Former friend, AJ! (She joined Paige's squad!)

She showed up at the door, said "hi guys", and started making these apology hand gestures at us. I rolled my eyes at her in the clear language that asked, "what are you doing here?" AJ buried her face into her hands, and Kylie(my real friend, well I think so anyway) kicked me hard enough to send her to jail and then whisper-shouted "Hayley!" in an attempt to stop me from falling for AJs unclear intentions. Why was she here when she had clearly joined the CAPGH and knew that I had not been invited or welcomed there?

I just shrugged my shoulders and was surprised when Kylie rolled her eyes at me in frustration then walked back into the house. There was no way I could trust AJ now, so I just shook my head and gently shut the door in her face. Let me get back into the house; I have to go and gather the little ones to make sure we leave in time for the 10 am registration.

Anyway, back to the beef. We went over to the Layndoor Hotel where mom had arranged tea with her friends, and we could register for the dance battle before 10am, which was part of the entry requirement!

Paige has decided that the actual battle would be next Saturday. We might as well practice now since it would be hard during the week with the little ones involved in so many activities!

Guess who we bumped into in the hotel reception? Jennie Puddington. The newest member of the CAPG. Paige's latest squad member snarled at Charlotte and said, " Hey Charlotte, you know there are punishments for quitting the CAPG right?" She then looked me up and down with an icy glare.

" More like she needs therapy from having been in the CAPG," I bellowed, narrowing my eyes and screwing my face. " Hanging out with people like you would do that to a girl! Anyways we have got to go. We do not want to keep the tiny's waiting. And by tiny's I mean award-winning children who have their mother as Xavia Degrange. See you at the dance battle next week!"

We had registered our names, and Paige and her crew need to know that we are not here to play.

Friday, July 11th

Today is the day, the day the birds sing and the clownfish chirp. Sorry, my writing is messy. This is because I am running from Paige, and I will be mortified if she catches me and grabs my diary. Then I will be well, Uhm, diaryless!

Someone told her that I have written about her in my diary and she wants to see what it is! As class president, she very craftily suggested that we play granny's keys. That game where a "mean, rude, self-entitled, snob" gets picked to be a thief. This thief must take the keys without getting noticed. Yeah, a similar scenario is happening here except instead of the keys, it's my DIARY that has been chosen for the golden prize, and that snob is Paige! Why did I bring it into school today? I have to find a way to get my diary out of this mess!

FINALLY, WE ARE DONE WITH THIS CHAPTER! YOU'RE RIGHT HARPER. I DID TAKE YOUR DIARY BUT ONLY BECAUSE I HEARD A RUMOUR THAT YOU HAVE BEEN SPREADING UNBELIEVABLE, INEXACT LIES ABOUT ME! I M JUST WRITING THIS MINI ENTRY TO WARN YOU NOW.

1I M GETTING BRAIDS IN MY HAIR TOMORROW, SO I'M GOING TO SLAY AT THE DANCE BATTLE. AND TBH, YOU ARE SOOO LAME. I'M TALKING ABOUT CHAHAL RENIS LAME! YOU KNOW THAT TV SHOW HOST WHO COULD NOT GET PEOPLE TO COME ONTO HER SHOW EVEN IF SHE PAID THEM! YES, THAT LAME. I HEARD SHE GOT SENTENCED TO A YEAR OF DOING VOICE OVER ON RUGRATS BY HER STATION BECAUSE HER RATINGS WERE SO POOR! YOU, HARPER, REPRESENT CHAHAL, YOUR FRIENDS ARE THE RUG RATS, AND WE ARE GOING TO TAKE YOU OFF THE CHARTS TOMORROW!

NOW THAT I KNOW YOUR PLOT, I NEED YOU TO KNOW THAT IT WILL NOT WORK! AND JUST IN CASE YOU FORGOT YOUR PLAN BECAUSE OF ALL YOUR OTHER *VILLAINOUS*

PLOTS, I'LL BE KIND AND REMIND YOU. I DON'T TRUST YOUR LITTLE SPY AJ ONE BIT! SHE'LL NEED TO PROVE HERSELF FIRST. SHE WILL NEED TO DO THAT BY DINGDONG (DOORBELL RINGS). ONE SEC, MY NEW DAILY UNIFORM HAS JUST COME IN! I MIGHT KEEP THIS LITTLE DIARY AT MY HOUSE FOREVER.   OOPS, I MEAN AT MY MANSION!

BTW I KNOW ALL ABOUT YOUR LITTLE ADVICE PLATFORM, HARPER HELPS! I MANAGED TO HACK INTO IT WITH YOUR PASSWORD HQ. AKA LOSER-SCENT. LIKE, WHO, WHO, WHICH PRISSY, PINK, PUKE PRINCESS USES THEIR INITIALS AS THEIR PASSWORD? TOMORROW I'LL BE ASKING AJ TO WRITE THE FIRST MEAN LETTER FOR HARPER HELPS IN YOUR DIARY! JUST TO BE PERFECTLY CLEAR, NO INFORMATION ABOUT THE CAPG'S (COOL AND POPULAR GIRLS) IS LEAVING THESE PRETTY, PUNCH SHADE LIPS. SO MUCH FOR WRITING DOWN YOUR SECRETS, I AM WELL ONTO YOU NOW AM GOING TO MAKE SURE MY GIRLS AND I DEFINITELY ROAST YOU AT THAT BATTLE TOMORROW!   GET USED TO LIVING IN MY SHADOWS!   YOUR AMBITION AS THE NEW

GIRL WANTING TO WALTZ INTO MY SCHOOL AND TAKE OVER, I AM DEFINITELY NOT HAVING THAT!

...TO BE CONTINUED

.

WANT TO SEE WHAT' S COMING NEXT. DIARIES OF A DRAMA QUEEN- ANYTHING TO WIN COMING OUT SOON!

About the Author

Ashirai Ndoro published this book at nine-years-old and has imagination and creativity that takes her on many wild and exciting adventures. A well-travelled year five student at a primary school in Buckinghamshire, England, she has visited ten countries over four continents so far. She hopes to see more of the world as well as incorporate different geographical settings in more of her stories in the future.

Her parents, although born in England, are of Zimbabwean and Nigerian descent, and she identifies strongly with her African culture. This is Ashirai's first book that she was keen to be out before her 10th birthday, and she just managed to achieve her goal.

Ashirai hopes to inspire other young children to pursue their passions and express themselves through writing, dance and acting.

Printed in Poland
by Amazon Fulfillment
Poland Sp. z o.o., Wrocław